To my Father
For whom all things were possible.

Lily Trezevant

RISING TO THE SURFACE

AUSTIN MACAULEY
PUBLISHERS LTD.

A CIP catalogue record for this title is available from the British
Library.

ISBN 978 184963 986 6

www.austinmacauley.com

First Published (2014)
Austin Macauley Publishers Ltd.
25 Canada Square
Canary Wharf
London
E14 5LB

Printed and bound in Great Britain

Prologue

Mid-winter 2008

Nearly mid-night: the doorbell rang at a time all should be silent.

Typical, thought Maria, Daniels's forgotten his key again. How on earth did he manage when he was away at university? No doubt relied on his housemates to let him in. She hadn't heard his bike roar up the drive but, tucked up in bed, she was engrossed in her book. Good job Matthew was downstairs watching *Match of the Day*.

Male voices. The fourth stair creaking as someone came up.

'Maria... Darling, I need you to come downstairs. Some police officers are here to talk to us.'

* * *

Chapter One

Early Spring 2009

The memories from the past were surely still there, piled up high like small wooden blocks in a game the children once played. Extract them carefully, one by one, so the tower doesn't fall down. Relive the happy times and remember joyous laughter.

There really was no way of knowing if this was the very worst it could get or would there be more to contend with in this long, long battle of exhausted emotions. Lying in a darkened room was never an option, but Maria had underestimated the Herculean effort needed just to get through each day. Ending up at the same point at which she started, there seemed little conceivable progress.

When a small sense of purpose returned, it was tightly

grasped – a welcome hand-hold on a vast, barren rock-face. Would it ever be possible to be objective and accept what had taken place? The crackle of electricity as mental pathways were re-connected could almost be heard as parts of her consciousness flickered into life again. Deep within, her reference points were still there and must be retrieved. The care and concern of others had never been far away, but fear of dragging them down meant keeping them at a distance. Slowly, slowly, confidence was returning and with it the desire to reclaim her life.

The luxury of time was something new. Being sensible and resourceful, Maria's days had always been full of activity and the adjustment to quiet contemplation took some getting used to. Medication blurred the edges and new directions presented themselves. Railing against injustice would achieve nothing but heap more sadness upon what was already there, so no feeling sorry for herself: keep moving forwards.

Within a short drive from where they lived were several lovely parks all with gardens, woodland walks and lakes. Maria loved to alternate her regular constitutionals in these parks.

The persistent rain of the past few weeks had refreshed the gardens and the walk down to the lake was full of vibrant colour. Thinking back to the days of small, scampering children, Maria walked and walked. Her daughter Francesca would never stray very far, but Thomas and Daniel would be off! It was always wise to put them in brightly coloured T-shirts so they could be spotted from a distance and their progress monitored.

Maria had used the full version of their names way beyond childhood and long after they had all succumbed to shortened forms. Not surprisingly, they had become Fran, Tom and Dan as soon as they had started school.

(Someone she had known at school had tried to call her Maz – but she quickly dispensed with that.)

In case the children took to the stage, she had wanted to give them semi-flamboyant second names but their father had put his foot down at suggestions like Crispin and Isadora.

Names have both good and bad associations. You would be unlikely to name your child after someone who was nasty to you in the playground or the class nerd. Surnames also need to be taken into account as some alliterations are too comical.

Some names never seem to date: documented in 'Genesis', Sarah, Rebecca and Rachel; Adam, Jacob and and Joseph are still popular today. Of course, some haven't stayed the course such as Shem, Ham and Japheth – the sons of Noah. Although Maria thought that the name Noah itself was making a bit of a comeback in recent times. She was surprised that Chloe was a biblical name for now in modern times it regularly came top in the most popular girls' names of the day.

Like hemlines and hairstyles, names go in and out of fashion. Eating her lunch in the park recently, she watched dear little twin girls of no more than two years old called Mabel and Iris playing on the swings. Maria would have been horrified to have been called either Mabel or Iris growing up in the 1970s but in allowing a generation or two to elapse, those names now seemed very sweet.

Names were so important – her father had once said it would endear you to someone if you were always to remember their name after a first introduction. How true: she was always flattered when someone remembered hers and then peppered conversations with it. It does make you feel special somehow.

It's strange that television programmes hardly ever have two characters with the same name. That's really not a reflection of true life for Maria remembered among her friends at secondary school there were three Dianas and four Annes. An assortment of nicknames distinguished one from the other.

Then there were the same names for both sexes, albeit with subtle differences in spelling: Lesley, Hilary, Robyn. The American trend for apparently using surnames as first names seemed to have caught on over here as the Taylors, Marshalls and Madisons bear witness to.

No, she had chosen well and hoped that Francesca, Thomas and Daniel were happy with their names as they grew up.

*

Seven ducks waddled up as she sat on a bench by the lake and stood agitating water droplets from their backs and stretching their wings. Some of them had one very curly tail feather. Why should that be? She didn't have to come up with an answer, unlike in days long gone when questions posed by Daniel demanded an immediate and fulsome reply. They settled down in what looked like the most uncomfortable of positions, with their heads turned completely backwards, beaks tucked under a wing. Eyes not quite closed, they stayed close by for quite a while, then sprang to life as Maria got up to continue her walk, quacking hopefully for food; but she was empty-handed.

A wonderful photo opportunity of two pheasants amongst the bluebells was marred by two fellow walkers coming into view. Perhaps the pheasants would still be there if she went back later? Don't worry: keep walking, there would be other lovely things to see along the way.

Underestimating the steep gradient of a hill, a well-placed bench was most welcome. A tall, sad man walked past. No eye contact or cheery good morning: he looked weighed down by grief and maybe he too had lost something precious.

Maria sat listening to the sounds around her – a distant waterfall; a plane overhead; birdsong; footfall on a wooden walkway; insects and camera shutters. Within stillness and peace there can be comforting, gentle noise. If you stop and listen you can hear it. Taking her notebook from her bag, she began to write down what she was thinking; how she was feeling. The counsellors said it may help. Words fell from her pen as her coffee went cold.

After a long time, Maria got up, quite stiff from the long sit-down on a hard bench. At what point in life did her hip and knee joints start to take time to get going? She couldn't remember a time when she would have just stood up and walked with fluid movements. That first walk downstairs each morning took quite a bit of concentration and effort; anyone watching would have added at least twenty years to her real age.

Round the next bend in the wooded path, she saw the Elephant Rock. The children's wonderfully vivid imaginations had named it such many years ago. Yes; it certainly did resemble the majestic head of a king elephant and, over time, had provided entertainment as a natural slide for thousands of small bottoms. She was amused to see how friction had worn away deeper trenches than when she last saw it.

At the entrance to the gardens, she had seen a poster advertising guided walks. A goodly number of people had taken up the invitation and were now standing by a gazebo which was draped in wisteria. The guide seemed to know his stuff, that much was true, but judging from the blank expressions on the faces of his audience, his words failed to spark appreciation. The group shuffled off slowly to have another tree or shrub reverently presented to them.

A party of school children taking part in an off-site activity day were much more animated, although they seemed more interested in the contents of their packed lunch than the flora and fauna around them. The teachers and parent-helpers were doing their best to inspire, but as their world was now dominated by electronics and hand-held consoles, the great outdoors must be somewhat bewildering. No matter; they would be back in front of their flat screens soon enough and their virtual world is real enough to them. In days gone by, Maria would have volunteered for such a school trip, although some of the boys looked quite a handful and that struck a chord.

The Walled Garden had always been a favourite place and

Maria sat on the bench dedicated to the Baker family. Throughout the gardens, it was touching to see how loved ones had been remembered by benches. In time, perhaps one would appear with her name on a brass plaque and she hoped that it could be placed near the Elephant Rock.

The sun shone and raised the temperature by several degrees. March had been unseasonably cold this year and it was lovely to feel the warmth of the sun's rays on her face.

The tour guide came into the Walled Garden with his entourage and she saw two ladies take their chance and make a bid for freedom round the back of the yew hedge. Wise move. Others with less gung-ho spirit were doomed to another monologue, this time about the myrtle bush she was sitting next to.

Solitary walks provided the chance to reflect and begin to untangle the chaos in Maria's head. It was the start of a long process – going backwards to come forwards and continue the journey. Was running away the only alternative to life as it had become?

Hide so as not to be found: craving total shutdown and dreamless sleep.

Although Maria was intelligent and her eloquence had seen her through many difficult scenarios, she couldn't seem to find the appropriate vocabulary to articulate an explanation for her actions that was in any way good enough.

She had raged against everything and everyone: her husband, caught in relentless crossfire, had tried and tried to convince her that the darkest hours are just before dawn, but her desperate night went on and on and on.

Having lost self-belief, she could not process his reassurances. Fragile and vulnerable, with little reserve left to cope.

Suspicion and paranoia had tested their love: grief, mistrust, confusion, communication breakdown had all caused raw and open wounds. How could they be healed?

On her own, Maria had begun the journey back within herself to retrieve her reference points, if they were still there, and begin to move forwards into the light. A crippling sense of foreboding was still cloaked around her and she needed so much strength to overcome the fear of what lay ahead.

Chapter Two

Late spring 2009

Life: it would flow gently by for years and years with nothing changing very much, then suddenly you'd be brought up short by so much happening at once. Like turbulent waves coming at her on a shoreline, Maria had been knocked down again and again.

'Take each day as it comes' was advice that was meant well, along with never knowing what the future holds. It's just as well life does only come one day at a time, for any more would surely be insurmountable.

With resourcefulness and self-reliance, Maria had steered a path through life for over five decades. Her children were a joy – affectionate and funny; so much laughter over the years. Unconditional maternal love had been rewarded by their achievements far exceeding her own, but in such different ways. Thomas and Daniel, intrepid and spirited young men, had seen more of the world than she ever would; Francesca, with such verve and confidence, had become a successful academic and was now all grown up and married. Maria wished for a grandchild before too long.

Sadly, it was now disconnection she craved. Just for a short while, she knew she couldn't be anything to anyone. Of course she would go home. It was where she belonged and she was still needed. Flying in the face of adaptation, she really just wanted everything to go back to as it was before. No change had been necessary: all had been going well. Struggling to accept that life would never be the same again had delayed any positive move forward and weighed down by so much sorrow, she had ceased to function properly.

This hotel near the sea was perfect; allowing her space to be anonymous and breathe again. Apart from a mild curiosity as to who it was in the helicopter that landed in the grounds yesterday, there was no desire to acknowledge anyone around her.

Peacocks were calling. Distinctive and mournful, their cries pierced the stillness of the late May morning.

Daniel, are you close by?

It was not usual for her to reject company and seek absolute solitude, but the closing down process was essential before a forward path could emerge. It hadn't happened yet. The sea was there to distract and yet help re-focus. How lovely to be allowed just to sit and contemplate for as long as she needed. No little children to drag her away to build sandcastles or buy ice-creams as in days gone by; but how Maria missed those innocent times.

No two scenes had been the same in the four visits she had made to the deserted beach. Will the tide be in or out? Will the waves be gentle or crashing? The vagaries and non-cooperation of real life could be a reflection of the sea and its moods. It's a mistake to guess what will happen next: wait and see.

Submerged by almost tangible grief as she had been for weeks now, Maria crunched her way across the pebbles, watching the waves. A girl adrift and forlorn.

Girl? She flattered herself; although perhaps tortuous emotions throw you back to childhood. A time when life was simple and she was taken care of; advised and guided well. You only seem to remember the sunny, happy days of childhood but it must have rained, sometimes.

If all your established reference points have been so totally eradicated, maybe regression was the answer; to go back and start all over again.

Daniel was beyond her reach in his darkest hour, dying alone on a cold deserted road.

The verdict of accidental death was in no way adequate. Maria needed to know how? Why? Where were the answers she desperately needed?

Familiar boundaries had been enveloped by the blackest shroud of confusion and hopelessness. So many memories and emotions had tumbled out of their special places in her heart and mind, leaving her raw and vulnerable. Reminding her of one of those old apothecary chests, with a hundred drawers for a hundred herbs. It had been knocked over and the boxes had fallen out, spilling their contents. Would the right herbs ever be put back in the right drawers? Some would; shut the drawer tightly to keep them safe.

*

Sitting on her own in a hotel courtyard with a glass of

champagne is not something Maria would normally have been comfortable with, for she would have interpreted the glances of strangers as pity for the poor woman with no husband or companions. They had no way of knowing that this was most definitely her choice, for Matthew had wanted to come with her. All her dear friends, so wonderfully kind and attentive, would have been with her too had that been what she needed, she only had to ask. Removing herself from well-intentioned concern gave them tacit permission to retreat beyond the probing analysis of conversation.

Should she try to write down her thoughts? Her counsellors said it may help.

Asking for paper and a pencil at reception, Maria returned to her table in the courtyard and began to write.

With no laptop or cold, stark product of the 21st century available to her, the graphite pencil is just fine; gratifyingly grounded, like the earth it came from. All those ancient atoms of carbon being formed into words to be read. It really was quite nostalgic to be writing her first story with the tool she would have first used in childhood. Going backwards to come forwards.

As the afternoon unfolds, her thoughts take shape and create the written word. After months of uncertainty, anxiety, loss of self-belief she thinks she may have something to create a platform for recovery. The experience is strangely cathartic; perhaps that could be the title of her work – Catharsis. Seems a bit pompous, so perhaps not.

One o'clock approaches. It really is very warm in the courtyard and she hears that clatter of plates and cutlery in the dining room. Strangely for her, she's not hungry, preferring to continue with her writing while the words flow freely. Completely absorbed with transcribing her thoughts, she's amazed how quickly time has passed.

*

There were signs in the hotel grounds advising guests not

to park under certain trees where the peacocks roosted at night. Judiciously Maria moved her car and later that afternoon, she went to look for them.

There were other birds in abundance – chaffinches, blue jays, ducks, pheasants. Four magpies: one for sorrow, two for joy, three for a girl and four for a boy. Yes, she'd experienced all of those over the course of time. Each time she walked down the private path to the sea, a robin threaded its way through the hedgerow alongside her. She remembered a friend once saying that within robins were spirits of the dear departed.

Daniel, is that you? Stay close to me.

Despite Maria's persistence, the peacocks were elusive: like the peace and resolution she was trying to find.

Chapter Three

Disorientated by waking up in a different room in a different bed without Matthew's comforting arm across her, it took a moment to remember where she was. Sleep hadn't been refreshing, as bubbles of confusion burst and released their contents in her unsettled mind. Fragments of dreams in which people past and present, in alternative scenarios playing different roles, morphed into each other. The last one had been so sad: of leaving somewhere without wanting to – a decision taken out of her hands. Tears she had cried in her sleep had pooled in her eyes.

The promise of another fine day slipped through a gap in the heavy curtains and enticed Maria out of bed to look at the gardens in the morning light.

Without noise or fanfare to herald their arrival, the peacocks were there.

One was on the wall beneath her window, the other on the ground. Turning a chair to face the open window, she watched with a lightening of spirit; mesmerised by their glorious indifference. How unique and captivating they were. The flash of bronze feathers when one of them spread their wings was unexpected and she smiled that something familiar could produce surprise.

What huge, beautiful birds they were.

Daniel, did you send them?

Dressing hurriedly, Maria went down into the gardens with her camera. They had moved but were both now side by side on another stone wall, preening and tantalising, untroubled by her presence. Hoping that they would show their magnificent tail feathers in all their glory, although she waited so patiently, there was no grand display. It didn't matter: Daniel had sent the peacocks to her and she was ready to go home.

*

The dear, anxious faces of Francesca, Thomas and Matthew were at the window as Maria pulled up on the drive. Had she done the wrong thing in going away on her own? The whole family were suffering, looking to her for guidance but she didn't have any answers for them.

'You OK Mum?' Thomas's gentle eyes searched for reassurance from Maria.

'I will be, my love.' She hoped that would be good enough for now. Francesca hugged her.

'We'll get through this together Mum – as a family.'

Matthew looked so lost and bewildered, struggling to find the right words to comfort his grieving wife. Of course, there were none.

'I've made a Shepherd's Pie,' said Francesca. 'I didn't want to do anything that Dan liked so we wouldn't think of him missing out.'

'Yeah,' Thomas chipped in, 'he always said it was just mush.'

Maria smiled at Daniel's siblings' take on things – she could learn from them. There was a beginning, a middle and an end to his life and it was right to talk about the Daniel they all had known. Her funny, exhausting and exasperating youngest child. Loud and active all his short life; keeping them entertained and amused with his antics and anecdotes.

Francesca and Thomas had put their own lives to one side while they coped with and processed this unimaginably and devastating tragedy. Now Maria must somehow show them that she was getting back on her feet. Once she had worked through her grief, she would be the mother they'd always known – she had to be, for they still needed their mother and always would.

This was real life and she had three children but one had died. She loved them and they loved her.

Chapter Four

Early winter 2007

The crowds moved with such focused purpose as Maria hurried across the concourse of Victoria Station from the underground. People criss-crossed each other at fast pace, dodging and weaving, performing last-second evasions with military precision. Looking up to check the departure board for her train while clasping at least three shopping bags in each hand, she increased her speed, thinking how annoying it was that the Sussex trains left from the furthest away platforms.

With much accomplished on her now traditional pre-Christmas shopping trip, her spirits were lifted as she thought ahead to the delight in the children's faces as they opened their gifts on Christmas day. She knew that Francesca and her new husband would be thrilled with the...

Thud...! air forced out of her chest... falling sideways to the ground... the hard impact of the station floor on her elbow... shopping bags dropping from her hands... in slow motion, the large glass bauble rolling away from its careful resting place on the top of a bag to be crushed underfoot...

'Oh my God! I'm so, so sorry; my fault completely. Are you all right? Here, let me help you. I'm so sorry. I didn't see you there.'

Strong arms lifted her to her feet as Maria did the only sensible thing and burst into tears.

Gulping down sobs, she gratefully acknowledged the kindness of strangers around her as her bags were gathered up and handed back to her – they could have easily made off with her precious packages.

'Please allow me to buy you a coffee – or something stronger. I'm so sorry.'

Looking up at her assailant/rescuer, Maria saw a kind, concerned face and, realising that she would probably miss her train, accepted his offer.

Carrying all her bags in one hand, he gently guided her to the nearest coffee shop.

'My name's Matthew.'
'Maria.'
'Hello Maria. What can I get you to drink?'

She watched Matthew as he waited at the counter to be served.

Height – tall, at least six foot.

Build – chunky, although that might have been due to his thick winter coat.

Hair – not much.

Age – not sure, mid-fifties? (Later, it turned out that she'd been a bit harsh, as he was only 49.)

Although it would have sensible to have checked the time of the next train, Maria was still feeling a bit dazed and doing a subtle 'body scan' to make sure there weren't any injuries. Apart from a very sore elbow, her bags must have cushioned the impact to a great extent – she hoped her purchases weren't damaged – and she was otherwise unscathed.

'He we are. I really can't apologise enough Maria.'

'Please don't worry. If a shattered bauble is the extent of the damage, I got away lightly.'

Conversation flowed easily as they chatted about what had brought them to Victoria Station at that time on that day.

Maria realised that she had by now missed the next train and probably the one after that.

'If it's not inappropriate to ask, I was wondering if you'd

like to have dinner with me?' Matthew had observed the absence of a wedding ring on Maria's hand.

'I'm sorry, but I do have to get home.'
'Yes, of course. I'm so sorry my clumsiness has delayed you.' Matthew was disappointed as he had really enjoyed the easy company of this attractive lady.
'Maybe if I give you my number you could get in touch.'

Did she actually say that? Maria was amazed by her confidence.

*

Matthew told her he loved her after just a few weeks after they had met, which in all honesty had overwhelmed her.

Unsure of what she really felt for him, she could not reciprocate his feelings. She had been on her own without a man for a very long time and thought she needed time to adjust to being part of a couple again. But as she was now approaching fifty (how did that happen?), why wait for slow development when time was precious and days may be numbered?

Anxieties and doubts that women in her situation must have the world over dominated her thoughts. Child-bearing and years of neglecting her body – and her body being neglected – made her self-conscious and hesitant about exposing it. Sexual desire had been suppressed for so long and she was unsure how she would respond to a man's touch again.

Oh but she wanted Matthew to make love to her. She knew he would take his time and be gentle with her; coaxing out of her a renewed feeling of being female and feminine.

For days before, the expectation of their love-making heightened Maria's senses and, with relief, she found her latent sexuality begin to re-emerge. She wanted to be with this man who so obviously desired her and that she could trust to enjoy her body as it was now.

The first time was glorious and exciting. Kissing was invitingly sensuous; lips gently touching between sips of champagne. Matthew took control and it felt good when he undressed her and Maria's fear at letting him see her near-naked body vanished as she gave herself to him, losing herself in his gentle touch.

She no longer felt self-conscious about what the advancing years had taken from her body as Matthew's tender caresses caused natural responses and her head was spinning with desire.

He lowered her down onto the bed and every nerve pulsed with electricity as his touch became focused and persistent.

Maria opened her eyes wide and looked up at him: a deep connection had been made.

This was the passion and excitement that Maria had been missing all these years: she wanted more and more.

Their relationship developed quickly and a delight in shared hopes for the future comforted Maria. They would have days out and holidays in the sun. Visits to the theatre and walks in the park. She had found a kindred spirit; someone with whom she could walk hand in hand into old age.

Just three months after knocking her flying at Victoria Station, Matthew asked her to marry him.

Of course she said yes.

Chapter Five

Early summer 2010

The first thing Maria did was buy a straw sunhat. It was a very long time since she had bought such a sensible hat but it was going to be hot in Majorca in June. Having dark brown eyes and olive skin, she had often been mistaken as being of Mediterranean origin and therefore should cope well in the sun; however, she disliked the feeling of being over-heated and would always seek cover. In any case, a few days sitting in dappled shade turned her nut-brown, much to the chagrin of others who laboured for that elusive honeyed-caramel tan.

It's true that blood of Portuguese, French and Indian descent ran through her, as discovered by her father many years ago when he researched their family tree. With more time to himself after retirement, he went back over several centuries, methodically and painstakingly assembling the branches which ended with her own three children – at least for the time being. He fully immersed himself in this extensive project, for he was genuinely interested in what his ancestry would reveal. Her mother was happy that it gave him a sense of purpose after many years working in the City – and kept him from under her feet!

Such a lot had happened since Matthew and she were last on this loveliest of islands. It was good to have made plans to return. The familiar little windmills greeted their arrival at the airport and the drive in their hire car to the south east of the island brought back happy thoughts of last year's holiday. It's obvious to her now, but there was no time to grieve for Lorna when she had died eight months ago, before events in Maria's own life spiralled out of control. The derailment from life by her own tragedy had been catastrophic, but she missed her friend so much.

No set guidelines for grieving were available – perhaps there simply weren't any. It was up to the individual to find their own process and rationale. Although maturity had equipped her with the ability to deal with many and varied situations, she was totally out of her depth. The question would be with her forever – how could she have prevented Daniel's death?

*

Valldemossa: Lorna had loved the little Majorcan mountain town. Maria remembered a conversation she'd had with her about favourite holiday destinations; she must go there and spend time in quiet contemplation, remembering her dear friend. The poignancy of Lorna's sheer determination and courage in battling her pernicious disease was not lost on those who knew and loved her. When her youngest son was safely on his way to university, there was no strength left in her to keep fighting for her family, and it was so very, very sad. There was no sense that could be made of the ending of such a vibrant and positive spirit, but hopefully a connection with Lorna's special place would be healing.

Under the shade of mimosa, laurel, olive and other trees beyond her arboreal knowledge, Maria stretched out on her lounger and looked up at the sky. The vapour trails of two aeroplanes had crossed directly above her, making a giant white kiss in the blue sky.

Is that from you Daniel?

The moon was also visible as a ghostly semi-circle, resembling one of those candied orange and lemon slices her mother only bought at Christmas; along with sticky dates and nuts in shells. It was probably the only time of year the sturdy nut-cracker was used and Maria could see her father now sitting in his armchair, newspaper in lap, cracking Brazil nuts for her and her younger sister.

Around the hotel pool were huge evergreen trees, echoing the festive theme in looking like fifty or more Christmas trees bunched up together, their cones effective as rustic baubles.

How long was it since she had last swum in the sea? Five years – maybe more. Swimming in spa pools makes you forget the sheer exhilaration of being buffeted by unpredictable waves and the buoyancy of salty water. She leapt around like a little girl when Matthew joined her in the clear, aquamarine water and she laughed as he swept her up and spun her effortlessly in his arms. Silvery fish swam around their legs and a cormorant preened itself on a rock. They watched with anticipation as it steadily prepared to take off majestically and soar into the sky; then collapsed in giggles as it flopped inelegantly into the sea! It surfaced with a look of 'I meant to do that' – but they weren't convinced.

With her feet still alarmingly swollen from the flight, swimming felt as if she had water-filled boots on – not a pleasant sensation at all. It looked most bizarre as they wobbled like blancmanges with each step she took as she walked back up the path to her lounger under the trees.

Revealed by the lack of clothing worn on the beach, tattoos – or 'body art' as the owners may prefer it called – were abundantly mesmerising in their patterns and size: that was just on the women she saw. When a pale, dumpy lady of a certain age turned away to present a large tattooed sun on her shoulder, Maria was so surprised!

Elaborate Celtic or tribal designs on young girls' lower backs were so prolific that she felt quite left out by not having one. It was strange to think that they have permanent symbols etched into their bodies that they wouldn't be able see properly without using mirrors. Maybe it was for the benefit of their lovers.

Ordinary dads sported exuberant sleeves of intricate inky designs from shoulder to wrist. Others had meaningful dedications to loved ones across their backs that she hoped weren't girlfriends or wives. Tattoos are expensive and painful to remove when love goes wrong. Both her sons had tattoos done in their late teens which, admittedly, she had mixed feelings about. Perhaps she felt it was a violation of the perfect little bodies she'd given them at birth. But what about having a small, discreet tattoo done when she got home? A reminder of survival and the hope for better days. Maria thought she might just do it – she really did.

Watching a small boy fill his bucket with sand before upending it to make a passable attempt at a castle and then stamping his foot on it brought back memories of holidays with her little ones. Eight-month-old Thomas's first experience with sand was to promptly put a spadeful in his mouth! He dribbled gritty spit for the rest of the afternoon. In their dining room at home, she had an enchanting photo of Francesca carefully carrying a precious bucket of sand back to the fortress she was building. Her sweet face a picture of concentration as her strawberry-blonde ringlets were blown by the breeze.

The pop of a bottle of Cava was a most welcome sound as the sun hit its zenith at noon. Lunch was all about resisting the lure of the extensive buffet and just having a light salad. Of course, the reality was a hugely satisfying feast after which followed a wine-induced siesta as Maria's troubles began to melt like chocolate in the Majorcan sun.

*

Later that evening, before Matthew resoundingly trounced her in a game of cribbage, she saw seven little girls parading in their newly acquired flamenco dresses. Daughters of holidaying friends, the little girls lined up on the terrace to have their photograph taken and fluttered their matching fans. As if on cue, the one lone brother in this ostentation of sisters appeared and proceeded to annoy all concerned by jumping off the wall behind them in the peculiar frog-like manner of small boys. Ignoring commands from his parents to stop, he carried on regardless, and Maria didn't miss the malevolent look in his eye! Maybe the toreador's outfit would have calmed his deliberate, attention-seeking sabotage of the joyous flamenco moment. He probably just felt left out.

Chapter Six

The next day, Maria suggested taking the catamaran on the Coastal Discovery trip. Seeing it arrive in their cove the day before, she thought it would be lovely way to see neighbouring inlets. It also had a glass bottom to observe marine life as they sailed along the coast. She recalled a tourist submarine trip taken on holiday with Thomas and Daniel before she had met Matthew. It was fascinating to view the secret world under the sea; watching the fish and sand eels weave in and out of billowing reeds.

Being prone to claustrophobia, Francesca had remained on terra firma and had her hair braided instead. Maria remembered it took absolutely ages to unbraid the many tiny little plaits before they went home and was very glad Francesca never was tempted to have it done again.

The decorative drawings of sea creatures on the sides of the catamaran reminded her of the bracelet Lorna had given her for her birthday a few years previously. Although chunky and a bit tricky to wear, it was made from sea green beads with nautical charms of anchors, starfish and shells. Maria resolved to wear the bracelet more often from now on.

*

The sun shone every day of their holiday and the temperature was just perfect. Hot but manageable during the day, cool at night for uninterrupted sleep. Maria's skin became lightly bronzed: the clinging dreary and damp spring had been sloughed off and something better was emerging.

However, failing to heed her words about the sensible and gradual building up of a tan, her resolutely Caucasian husband threw caution to the four winds and went for the burn on day one. Putting his faith in the Once-a-Day sun-cream, bought at vast expense at the airport, he lay out in full sun for most of the first day – and got burnt.

Of course he didn't feel it at the time. It's only as night falls that the pouring-acid-into-an-open-wound agony manifests itself and the pain hits without mercy.

How he must have regretted not taking her advice.

The following days saw her lovingly rubbing a soothing balm on his lobster-red torso and then, with admirable restraint, she held back the urge to slap his back in a 'There you go mate' way that's so hard to resist – it really is!

By coincidence, Matthew's cousin and her husband were also going to be in Majorca at the same time, with their holidays overlapping by three days. It was duly arranged that Matthew and Maria would drive across the other side of the island and collect them from their hotel in Illetes, before they would all go to Valldemossa for the afternoon.

After a sustaining breakfast from the all-you-can-eat buffet (Matthew was certainly out to do himself justice) they gathered a few essentials and set off in their hire car.

The trip began well enough: companionably pointing out fluffy clouds resembling dogs, ducks and maps of the British Isles – it's amazing how often you see one like that.

However, with hindsight, it would have helped if Matthew had taken more time to produce a clear and concise set of directions. Instead, five minutes before they left, he thrust a scrappy piece of paper at her with indistinct village names and road numbers making no sense at all.

It would also have helped if he had actually listened to her as she tried her very best to decipher his hastily produced instructions and kept on the motorway rather than branching off to the right.

Why would he do that? After all, she was only reading back to him his own directions.

They ended up in a small nondescript town with no obvious road signs, and then he asked:

'Which way now?'

Which way now??

What was she – Sat Nav made human??

The atmosphere got frostier and it was nothing to do with the super-efficient air-conditioning in the car.

After many wrong turns and not a few cross words, they finally ended up back on the main road. However, it wasn't long before Maria realised that they were heading back in the direction they had come.

With no obvious exit in sight and no hope of being in Illetes by midday – or any time soon – a phone call to his cousin resulted in the visit being cancelled with the agreement that they would meet up back in England later that summer.

Sadly, it also meant abandoning their trip to Valldemossa, but she knew that if Lorna was looking down on their failed attempt, she would have roared with laughter at their incompetence. After all, they were intelligent people and it was only map reading.

Never mind, there would be other chances to reschedule their visit later in the holiday: it was only a postponement.

Trying to salvage something of the trip, they stopped at the faded hill town of Montuiri. There were so many windmills striking the landscape; testimony to the town's former agricultural glory. But unfortunately there wasn't much else to see or do.

They drove on to Manacor, famous for its artificial pearl factories. That might be more interesting: maybe she would be treated to a little trinket if she was lucky.

Parking up, they went into what was purported to be a factory discount shop where they were immediately accosted by a gimlet-eyed sales assistant. A quick glance at the price tags revealed that the 'trinkets' were prohibitively expensive (300 euros for a very average looking necklace), so they beat a hasty retreat.

Back in the comfort of their hotel, several glasses of wine restored harmonious relations and muted the disappointment of not reaching Lorna's special place.

Recognition that a warm affinity with Lorna had been present throughout the holiday made Maria think that perhaps this was indeed a kind of grieving. That – and the acceptance of what is inevitable for us all.

*

Since their arrival in Majorca, the temperature had steadily increased and was now in the high twenties: she had been glad of her sunhat. With no room in her suitcase to take it home, she asked a newly arrived guest if she would like it, suggesting that they also pass it on to someone else on returning home.

The image of her sunhat being circulated to hotel guests all summer long was just lovely and of leaving something in the place where she had been close to Lorna.

Chapter Seven

Late summer 2011

'Mice have been at my cricket pads...' a disembodied voice from the loft cried out. '... and there are droppings everywhere!'

This really didn't bode well.

Matthew's preparations for his first cricket match in over two years had begun somewhat inauspiciously and Maria, suppressing her amusement, found it hard to be sympathetic. His old cricket team from Little Crendon were 'on tour' in their corner of Sussex and, much to Matthew's delight, were one player short for their Saturday fixture in a nearby village. Was he available? Too right he was. Oh to relive his glory days of yore.

Let the preparations begin!

A cool box was needed. To chill an isotonic drink or a light bite for lunch? No; for the ice packs and the Deep Freeze spray. He really was taking this very seriously.

'I'll see if the gym instructor knows some good exercises for thigh management and knee flexibility,' said Matthew over a large portion of steak and mushroom pie that evening. Hmm, thought Maria, might take a bit more than that to hone his body in readiness for the big day.

She loved his body just as it was: big, strong and so reassuring to have folded around her at night. Glad he had come into to her life in the autumn of her days; she would have loving companionship in the winter that followed.

'No alcohol for me Sweetheart.'
Had she heard him correctly?

Each evening saw him assiduously watching the weather forecast which didn't exactly fill him with glee. After a mild and dry spring, which prompted local government to impose a hosepipe ban, summer had been a real washout. It had made Maria smile when she overheard someone in the Post Office queue say, 'Well, this is the wettest drought I've ever known.'

Matthew was really looking forward to seeing his old team mates again. They were an interesting mix of ages and ethnicities, as revealed by their names: Arthur, Wayne and Rajan were just three of the merry band. All had something in common – a love of cricket and an enjoyment of the camaraderie a team sport generated. She knew that Matthew had missed his weekend cricket after moving down to Sussex to be with her and recognised his need to be part of the gang.

Growing up in the foothills of the Himalayas, her father had been an excellent cricketer and played for the India schoolboys team for several seasons. Although he was now in his late eighties, he still remembered The Bodyline Tour of 1932 and the team visiting his school for practice matches on their way out to Australia. He says he opened the batting with Douglas Jardine which may have been true. However, with his advancing years, his memory is somewhat hazy for now he says he also opened the batting with Don Bradman, Lindsay Hassett and other cricketing luminaries!

This rivalled the tale of his school-boy assault on Mount Everest when he says he reached 22,000 feet. However, the tale was hugely exaggerated over time, with him going higher and higher until he got to 32,000 feet. Sadly, Everest is 29,000 feet high, so her father was scaling thin air by the end!

He was convinced that he was one of Sir Edmund Hillary's expedition but the dates didn't quite match up, for her father would have been living in England for over five years by the time Everest was conquered in 1953. It made a lovely story though and no-one had the heart to question his triumph. Maria and her sisters would say that, when their father departed this earth and they were going through his effects, wouldn't they feel awful on reading a letter from Sir Edmund saying, 'Great having you with us at the summit'?

They would feel even worse to read one from Don Bradman saying, 'A cracking century! Glad you were part of the team.'

The cricketing gene was obviously passed down to Maria's sons. Although Daniel was early teenage when he first showed any interest in the game, he was an absolute natural and quickly became the star player at school. With the confidence of youth he sent fours and sixes flying all over the pitch with the fielders having to scurry round like squirrels trying to retrieve the ball. Maria was thrilled to have been watching when he scored his first century and she was touched that he immediately turned to her and raised his cricket helmet in salute, as if to say, 'That was for you Mum.'

They still talk about how one huge six broke a library window. One of his teachers sitting near her in the pavilion said of her not exactly academic son, 'Well, that's the biggest impact Dan's had on the library all year.' How true.

Maria used to rush at life as if it was a race to be completed as quickly as possible in case time ran out. Now her days evolved at a much less frantic pace. This had taken some getting used to, for as far back as she could remember, there was a job for every minute of the day. Maybe it was the fear of failing that constantly pushed her forwards, or the satisfaction that she mostly achieved all that she set out to do each day – what extraordinary self-discipline.

Caught out by the hot sunshine after a very chilly start to the day, Maria overheated as she tramped through the Memorial Gardens to the shopping Mall. Setting off that morning in boots and raincoat, she now wished she had worn sandals and something floaty. However, looking at the dark grey clouds in the distance, maybe the boots had been a good idea – she knew the tricks the English weather likes to play. Rushing to get the shopping done and run her errands she was looking forward to retreating to her new sanctuary – the spa.

Over many years, visits to a 16th century country hotel had created wonderful memories of happy days with family and friends. Matthew had thought it would be the perfect venue for their wedding reception – and it had been. Although the hotel had met fierce opposition from local villagers for their plans to build a spa, their plans were finally approved.

Going to the spa gave her permission to relish solitude and create a carapace of peace around her. Headphones in the gym were a signal that she didn't wish to engage in conversation; swimming could be naturally solitary without being rude. As both the indoor and outdoor pools were connected and kept at the same temperature, she had swum outside even in late January. Taking care of herself had moved higher up the priority ladder for she knew that if she could stay calm and grounded, then she would be better placed to think on her feet and be there when needed.

*

The big day dawned and our cricketing hero was primed and ready for action!

'I'm off to Pilates my love,' Maria called out as she left Matthew gathering various strapping supports and all manner of embrocation necessary for the challenge that lay ahead.

'OK darling. David's picking me up. I'll text you when I know if we're batting or fielding first.'

On the many occasions that she had watched a cricket match, Maria realised that most of the time nothing much really happened and when it did, she was invariably looking the other way. She'd better try to be more observant this afternoon.

Still amazed that the gentle Pilates movements left her hot and really quite worn out, Maria checked her mobile to see that Little Crendon were batting first and, as Matthew was way down the batting order, she thought that she had plenty of time to go home and shower. Sadly, that turned out to be a little optimistic.

As she arrived at the delightful little cricket ground tucked away at the end of an old Sussex lane, the rainclouds had parted to reveal a lovely English summer's afternoon. The pitch seemed to be set in a natural basin surrounded by mature oak trees with a stream running close to one side. She wondered how many wayward balls had ended up in there over time. Armed with her deckchair, newspaper, book and picnic, she set up camp by the stream.

But where was our cricketing legend? In fact, where were any of the players?

Checking the scoreboard gave her the answer. Little Crendon were bowled out for 87 – oh dear. Still, maybe Matthew had saved the team from total humiliation by coming to the crease and putting on half a century. That would be really something: she could hear him now recounting the tale for years to come.

She found the troops in the pavilion – which was rather a grand name for the ancient hut, which would have collapsed long ago if it weren't for the extensive network of cobwebs holding it together. They were hunkered over the cricket tea, looking glum.

'Hi everyone.' Maria tried to be cheery and upbeat. 'How did you get on?'

Matthew gave the thumbs down and sank his teeth into an egg and cress sandwich. Lifting his left arm up revealed a large plaster on his elbow and a trail of dried blood running down to his wrist. Bruising had already started and his whole lower arm was quite swollen.

'Thought it was broken at first. Peter's checked it out and thinks it's OK.'

It transpired that Peter was an equine vet so Maria wasn't convinced that the diagnosis could be relied upon, but Matthew seemed satisfied.

'How did it happen?' she asked.

'Tripped up coming out of the pavilion on my way to bat. Those bloody mice had chewed through the straps of my pads.'

Wisely, Maria retreated to her camp before her mirth could no longer be contained and, quite content with her own company, settled in for the afternoon.

As there was no way he could field with one arm, Matthew was relegated to the scorers' table with Wilf from the opposing team.

It wasn't going to be the start of a warm and lasting friendship as Wilf spent more time talking about his assorted ailments and pacemaker than keeping his eyes on the match. Not that he would have been able to see very much anyway through his grime-coated spectacles.

When Maria kept her poor wounded husband company for a while, the only exchange of conversation he had with Wilf was to question the scoring.

'Was that a four?'

'No Wilf, just two runs,' said Matthew, stifling his

impatience with a grimace at Maria.

'So that takes the total to 47.'

'Well, I make it 44 Wilf. Perhaps you should check again.'

The gentle noises of village cricket and the burbling stream soothed Maria as she relaxed back in her deckchair and enjoyed the evening sun of a late summer's day. A little white feather fluttered down from the tree's canopy and landed on her shoulder.

Hello Daniel: my own precious angel

Although she did feel just a little sorry that Matthew had been robbed of his glorious return to the game he loved but if a graze on his elbow was his only injury, he should count himself lucky.

'I'm starving,' he said as they drove home. 'That cricket tea wouldn't have satisfied a flea. Let's pick up a take-away.'

'Good idea,' said Maria.

That bottle of Sauvignon Blanc that she had smuggled in had gone down very well throughout the afternoon and had given her quite an appetite too.

Chapter Eight

Summer 2012

Much to her surprise, Maria was really enjoying the summer Olympics. Even though she had done her utmost to get out of anything connected with running, jumping or throwing things at school, living in England in 2012 you couldn't fail to be caught up in the lengthy preparations and increasing excitement of what was about to happen. The opening ceremony was truly spectacular and our success in the games that followed, signified by Team GB's mounting tally of medals, was tremendous.

Maria had also enjoyed the Diamond Jubilee celebrations and, unsurprisingly, that year had turned out to be immensely patriotic. To use a hackneyed phrase, she felt proud to be British. The sight of their redoubtable Queen braving the wind and rain of a typical English summer's day as the Royal barge made its way along the Thames was incredibly moving. In her silver and white outfit, our lovely Monarch looked like the pearl in an oyster. Refusing to sit in the specially commissioned thrones, she steadfastly remained standing for hours, defying the elements to get the better of her and putting her own comfort aside to ensure that her public would have the best view of her as the floating Jubilee Pageant went past.

What stoicism; she could teach the next generation a thing or two about fortitude and selflessness. Maria hadn't yet found an answer to the question of how so many adolescents were missing these commendable qualities – they should try being Queen for a week.

Of course, June should have started with warm, sun-filled days; the forerunner to a long hot summer. But this was the UK and, by dint of our birth, we abandon all hope of meteorological good fortune. Instead, we are adept at making the most of what comes our way or else our plans would be on permanent hold. So, up went the bunting and we got on with the show.

'Shall we canvass opinion for a street party?' said Matthew over breakfast.

He obviously hadn't had one in whatever street he was living in at the time of the Silver Jubilee in the late seventies, thought Maria. What a disaster that had been, costing her mother the friendship of several neighbours in Oakwood Drive. Who would have thought that sensible women would have got so territorial over vol-au-vents and trifles.

'Well, that would take some organising and Jubilee Day is next Tuesday,' said Maria, secretly very relieved that Matthew hadn't had the idea in January. She had no wish to cajole/bully/press-gang her neighbours into providing essential requisites for a street party that was bound to end in fractured friendships.

'Ah that's true,' said Matthew. 'I do feel we should celebrate in some way though. After all, this is the only Diamond Jubilee we'll be around for.'

'Thanks for the reminder,' she replied.

Knowing she had to think quickly before he came up with another plan which would involve time and effort on her part, Maria was glad she remembered seeing a special Jubilee lunch advertised at a local restaurant and desperately hoped they had a vacancy.

Earlier that year, as his internet skills improved, Matthew spent ages doing online research on destinations for their summer break, coming up with a two-centre holiday in North Wales. Both hotels sounded lovely, set in extensive grounds with their own spas and near the coast for bracing seaside walks.

Summer holidays had revolved around children's basic requirements for sandy beaches, safe swimming and amusement arcades for so many years that putting her needs first still took some getting used to.

By the time the children were planning their own holidays with their friends and partners Maria was more than ready to self-prioritise, having had her fill of sitting on wet Cornish beaches in her cagoule, building sandcastles for hyperactive little ones.

'We'll be driving up near Worcester,' Matthew said as he looked up from the UK road atlas he'd spent the last hour perusing: maps can be quite hypnotic. 'We can visit your old school friend in her country pile.'

Many years before, Julia had converted to Buddhism and was now called Dharmadhatu. Living in the sticks, she was part of the community team running a retreat called Samadhi Sutta.

As she learned more about the religion, Maria envied Julia's tranquil, non-judgmental and unhurried lifestyle. Meditation must be a wonderful tool to use to escape to a quiet oasis in an increasingly frantic world. However, on the occasions she had tried to meditate, she always ended up wondering what she was cooking for dinner and whether there was enough in the laundry basket for a whites wash. Maybe hers was a mind that couldn't be diverted by contemplative thought. Might be worth trying again; anything to keep on an even keel.

Packed and ready to go, they set off on a dreary early August morning towards Wales with Maria hoping that (a) she'd remembered everything and (b) Julia's directions were easy to interpret from Worcester.

All went well and after following the directions meticulously, they made a right turn off the main road by a large pile of bricks ('Don't ask' was Julia's aside in the directions) and entering a narrow, unmade lane. This they followed for well over a mile, with Matthew grumbling about what the pot-holes were doing to his suspension.

Fields of wheat and poppies lay on either side, with more fields around them as far as they could see. The scenery was captivating, with only the sights and sounds of nature coming at her through the open car window.

'Well, good job those directions were thorough,' said Matthew. 'This really is off the beaten track. You would never have got me here with the just the road map, my love.'

Maria let the gentle dig at her navigating skills pass unchallenged but thought that he was becoming a little critical of late when she only ever did her best.

The retreat was set in several acres of rambling woods and fields, with a water meadow full of wild flowers sloping down to a stream. Immediately, there was a wonderful feeling of calm and of time slowing down which Maria knew she would relish.

After a frugal lunch which centred around sprouting seeds (which would probably play havoc with Matthew's digestive system) and lentils (which definitely would), Julia took them on a leisurely walk through the gardens and fields to the stream.

The water meadow was bursting with marsh marigolds, ragged robin and forget-me-nots, all intermingling with the grasses and rushes. Huge dragonflies hovered and dipped over the reeds; honeybees sought nectar amongst the most brightly coloured flowers and butterflies floated dreamily throughout the peaceful scene.

Environmentalists were keen to sustain indigenous flowers that Maria wondered if a corner of their garden could be turned over to Mother Nature and evolve into a small meadow of British wild flowers? Having signed up to a 'Gardening for Beginners' course that autumn, she felt really motivated to investigate further.

As they walked back, a sudden shower fell through the sunshine creating a rainbow over the water meadow behind them. Maria could see no clear boundary where one colour ended and another began. There was just a beautiful bright blending of violet, indigo, blue, green, yellow, orange and red: a celestial picture just for her.

Daniel, did you draw it?

*

Late afternoon, they reluctantly departed from the peace and serenity of Samadhi Sutta to drive up to Colwyn Bay

'I'm so looking forward to seeing the hotel,' she said as they zipped along a surprisingly empty motorway. 'Can't wait to see the spa and have a swi… oh no.'

'What is it?' Matthew said.

'I've forgotten my swimming costume,' Maria said sheepishly. Bracing herself for an insufferably smug reply from Matthew, she was quietly pleased when he said, 'Oops – so have I!'

They decided to swing off the motorway and look for a superstore, hopefully finding something appropriate. The selection was somewhat limited and, as Maria didn't have the luxury of shopping around, she grabbed a boring black one-piece for herself and a jaunty multi-coloured pair of beach shorts for Matthew that she knew wouldn't impress. Well, it was a case of beggars can't be choosers and it was unlikely that he'd see anyone he knew in the wilds of Wales to mock his sartorial inelegance.

After checking in and being shown to their room, Matthew was thrilled that the hotel, chosen by pot luck, was very clean and comfortable. True to form, the first thing he did was pick up the remote and put the television on. Did all men do that or was it just him?

Perhaps she did what most women did and that was check out the freebie toiletries in the bathroom!

Kicking off his shoes, he flopped onto the super-kingsize bed and opened a bottle of wine ready to catch up on the day's events at the Olympics.

So different to recent times, Maria thought; for not so long ago, curtains would have been drawn, clothes thrown off before falling into bed and ecstatic love-making. She was disappointed – at what point did his compliments become less frequent and she felt less loved?

The next day they ventured to a nearby coastal town which a local magazine suggested was 'the jewel in Wales' crown.' To Maria's amusement, she wondered what influence the writer had been under to come up with such a complimentary review for the town they saw was tacky, tired and had definitely seen better days.

'Well that was a grim waste of time,' Matthew said.

Cutting their visit short, they drove along the coast for a while before turning inland and finding a delightful country pub for lunch.

After placing their order, Matthew brought the drinks over.

'Rubbish selection of beers.'

He was grumpy today, not like him at all – withdrawn, as if his mind was elsewhere.

'Everything OK sweetheart?' she gently enquired. 'Only you seem pre-occupied with something.'

'Yes, I'm fine. Don't know what you mean.' His reply was snappy; perhaps he was just hungry.

After an unacceptable wait, when the food finally did arrive, Matthew moaned that his chips were cold and the meat was tough.

He really was out-of-sorts today.

Moving on from Colwyn Bay, they drove through the wildly beautiful Snowdonia National Park and across the Menai Bridge into Anglesey. Once again, Matthew prided himself in finding a superb hotel for their second stay. More of a country manor house really, it boasted huge rooms, a dramatic staircase and galleried landings. The gardens were punctuated with contemporary sculptures and the views were incredible. More importantly, the weather continued to be kind and it was proving to be exactly the peaceful and restorative holiday they both needed.

*

Such hope for calmer waters was soon to evaporate, for Maria had no way of knowing that the storm clouds had gathered and her world would implode again…

Chapter Nine

Early winter 2012

Raw emotions are irrational: they don't yield to reason and if Maria could not understand the force of illogical fear, she could not begin to explain the disintegration of self.

Counselling and medication were still her crutches: she was supposed to be making progress so regression was not part of the plan. Although she was trying, it was so hard to move forward into a life without Daniel.

*

How had this happened? Why could she not see the warning signs until it was too late?

Texts beeping on his mobile at strange times; hushed phone calls in other rooms; the hastily minimised screen on his computer; late evenings at work.

Suspicion and paranoia made her confront Matthew. His words were hollow:

'You've been so distant and remote... I have suffered too... someone from work... only the once... it didn't mean anything... it's you I love...'

Black rage and all-consuming anger had descended; her absolute rejection of him was swift and brutal. How could he have risked everything that they had built up together for a transient, meaningless thrill?

Grief on top of grief had frozen Maria in bewildering self-inflicted isolation, but if it had to happen, the short days and long dark nights of winter were a small comfort and brought out in her some long-buried primeval instinct to almost hibernate. The season granted permission to hide from conflict and withdraw from a life that had become alien and exhausting.

Maria had no desire to seek company or conversation: the stark realisation that the only person she now needed was the one she had forced away. Could she forgive him? Was it possible their marriage could be saved? Anxious to break down the very barriers she had put up, she reached out to Matthew before more hurt and needless actions drove them further apart.

*

Green Park held no special memories for them – yet. After so many years of disciplined time-keeping, it was no surprise that she was early. Sunshine at this time of year did not take away the chill of the day but it was lovely to look up at a clear blue sky in December. Buying a coffee to warm up, she walked round this small London park, down to Buckingham Palace and up the other side, hearing the constant drone of the Park Lane traffic.

Sitting on a bench near the fountain of the girl and greyhound where they had agreed to meet, she looked at the people walking through the park around her and wondered what their purpose was that day.

Rays of a watery sun cut through the bare winter trees as she watched and waited. She felt anxious and tense, wondering how it would be when they saw each other again. Anger and grief could block the smiles; hope would falter. Bereft by the sudden changes life had imposed upon her, she missed saying 'we' and wanted to go home. But where was home now?

Recognising the hat that she'd bought him on another cold winter's afternoon, she saw Matthew arrive. Relieved that he had decided to accept the olive branch by agreeing to meet her; she was so, so glad to see him again. Slowly she walked towards him and wondered if he could sense that she was close by.

He turned and saw her but their greeting was awkward and his kiss barely touched her face. The loss of something precious seemed to hang in the air between them and, after many weeks apart, there was hesitation in their stilted first words face-to-face.

*

Maria remembered they walked through the park towards Shepherd Market – one of London's secrets, for she hadn't known it existed until recently. She was caught unawares when Matthew said that it felt wrong not holding her hand before taking her hand in his. Through the gloves they were both wearing, she felt a slight warmth; a small comforting connection that seemed like the first step on the long journey home.

Knowing it would be inappropriate to begin talking with depth and meaning, conversation was polite and enquired gently about their respective parents and children; their jobs and mutual friends. Entering an old London pub bedecked with garish Christmas decorations, Matthew ordered a bottle of wine and they found a quiet corner and, with a hesitance that was understandable, Maria began to speak.

Desperately hoping that she was choosing words to help him realise that her self-control and resilience was coming back: that she was conveying how the sense of foreboding that had been with her for months and months was beginning to disperse. She told him that she accepted her part in alienating him and was trying to rationalise his infidelity. They could work through this, she knew they could. Matthew listened quietly but his expression gave no indication that her words were reaching him. His eyes reflected deep hurt and mistrust; Maria felt a sense of hopelessness that she had left it too late to build bridges and now there would be no way forward.

They left the pub and found a small Italian restaurant. They must have ordered and eaten a meal, but Maria had no recollection of what it was. Matthew was beyond her reach and the afternoon was suffused in quiet sadness.

*

Following their afternoon in Green Park, they had exchanged tentative emails and phone calls. Matthew said he still loved her but was that the same as being in love? She was unable to second-guess how he now defined love. Maria was confused and searched for more explicit signals that their marriage wasn't beyond repair. With relief, she remembered that Matthew had been wearing his wedding ring; she had no intention of removing hers – the visible sign of their union was so important to her.

It was so obvious that the avalanche of grief which had engulfed them continued to weigh heavily. There were no landmarks for guidance and no experience to draw on. Stumbling around in darkness, they had fallen further and further apart; she was trying so hard to find her way back to him but it seemed impossible. Matthew was evasive and non-committal but Maria knew she must convince him to see her again.

Chapter Ten

Late winter 2012

Revealed by the bare branches of trees against the December sky, Maria noticed huge clumps of mistletoe as her train passed through fields and forests on her way to meet Matthew.

Realising that she was experiencing real excitement about seeing him again – a feeling that had gradually become submerged as thrilling first encounters gave way to established daily routine. She knew it had been right to persuade him to see her again and wanted so much to re-ignite the passion they once shared.

With no way of knowing whether it would be temporary or permanent, Matthew had returned to the town where he had been living before they met. Sensing his caution about seeing her again, Maria asked if she could come to him and although he doubted what purpose it would serve, nevertheless he agreed.

Making her travel arrangements, she hoped that she hadn't coerced him into something he didn't want or need. Dispelling such negative thoughts, she had to be resolute that it was the right decision: he was still her husband and there was still a chance for them.

As the train neared her destination she saw the red kites wheeling in the sky as if to announce her arrival. She remembered Matthew pointing them out to her on one of her first visits to stay with him, saying the rare birds had been re-introduced to the county and were now a thriving population. It seemed so long ago that she had last taken this train journey. How would she feel seeing more familiar sights? Of being in the town where romance had blossomed and he'd asked her to marry him?

Checking into the hotel, Maria smiled as the receptionist tried to engage her in small talk as to the purpose of her visit. She gave nothing away: nobody knew about her coming to see Matthew. This interlude had to be completely private for she would not have welcomed well-meaning advice from family and friends warning her against such foolishness.

The hotel room was truly bizarre: Maria had never seen such an odd collection of ugly, mismatched furniture. The receptionist said the room was an upgrade to the honeymoon suite; hopefully newlyweds would be too busy having rampant sex on the kingsize bed than puzzling over the outdated chaise longue, pseudo 'art-deco' mirrored chest of drawers and strange wardrobe under the eaves. It was also very odd not to have a door on the en suite.

Christmas lights glowed down the high street as she walked slowly to their meeting place and, once again, she experienced the stirrings of impatient excitement; the feeling a young child would have on the days before their birthday or on Christmas Eve.

She knew she would be early but wanted the heightened feeling of expectation as she waited for Matthew

The charming centuries-old pub was still the same and it didn't feel at all strange to be back there again.

Maria bought a bottle of wine and, finding a quiet table, sat down to wait for Matthew.

*

Time-keeping had never been one of his better attributes, but she knew he would come.

As when they had met in Green Park, Matthew was guarded: his kiss perfunctory, his smile not reaching his eyes. He pulled out a chair opposite her and sat down.

Although they talked for an hour or more, his decision was made. There was no going back and he needed to make a new life for himself, without the drama of walking on eggshells every day.

Seeing that he had taken his wedding ring off, she knew the end had come.

Maria spent the night alone in the hotel, leaving early to make the sad journey home.

Chapter Eleven

Early summer 2013

'Bumble! Bumble, get away!'

From her unseen place on the porch, Maria wondered why the black labrador was being called away from his beach discovery with such urgency. She could see a dark shape lying on the pebbles, larger than a dead fish or seagull. After lunch and her siesta, she would investigate.

The beach house on a vast stretch of Sussex coastline was everything Maria had hoped for, living up to the review in the magazine – unlike write-ups of previously visited holiday homes where optimistic words had promised much but furnished little. This was exactly the calm, peaceful seaside retreat she needed to help the ongoing healing process: nearly there…

First impressions were enchanting: bleached wooden floors, minimal decor and a colour palette of white and pale blue. Views from the front windows tracked the coastline through 180 degrees, from east to west, and all Maria could see were beach, sea and sky.

Poignantly, the rustic wooden dining table was set for two, but Matthew wouldn't be with her. She had tried again to convince him there was still a chance for them but exhaustive efforts to stabilise their marriage had failed. That chapter of her life was now closed: she had found the strength to move on and life was manageable – just.

Putting the second place setting to one side, she sat down with her lunch and a glass of wine. It felt all right – being on her own at the beach house. Both Francesca and Thomas said they could take time off work to come with her but she wanted to show them that she could do this.

She was alone but not lonely and welcomed the quiet solitude.

Maria watched the seagulls through the open French windows. After a while, she saw that there seemed to be a noticeable repetitive movement, with them flying almost vertically upwards to a height of about five metres then dropping something from their beaks which landed with a 'tock' on the shingle. They would then swoop down to find it.

What were they doing?

With incredible ingenuity, Maria realised that, with incredible ingenuity, they were cracking open cockles and clams that had been stranded by the receding tide! Much to her amusement, she saw that the downward swoop had to be at great speed for, seagulls being seagulls, there was always some lazy opportunist close by to intercept and grab the smashed shellfish for themselves.

Their antics kept Maria entertained for a long time before the combination of a long drive and the wine meant siesta time.

In the upstairs bedroom, the huge bed had a four-poster frame made of drift wood, crisp white cotton sheets and numerous pillows to snuggle around. It didn't take Maria long to fall asleep, with the soft sound of distant waves creating a nautical lullaby. Sleep came more easily to her now, unlike the distressing, fretful nights of recent times. Embracing all suggestions of help, she had genuinely found that yoga, deep breathing techniques, massage and other grounding therapies had made a real difference to her recovery.

Permission had been granted to focus on herself; to let go of despair and unresolved angst; to be allowed to gently rise to the surface.

Just to be able to be: just be.

Although she knew this beach quite well, Maria had forgotten the extreme variation in the high and low tides and wondered what the whooshing, crashing sound she could hear when she woke up. Stepping out onto the balcony, she saw that the tide must have raced in while she was sleeping, creating a very different coastal scene from when she had arrived. She hoped the sea hadn't covered whatever it was that had intrigued Bumble earlier, but the dark grey mass was still visible.

She watched the people on the beach, happy that the sun shone for them. Of course, they would have still been there in the damp and drizzle – buckets and spades at the ready. Resolutely finding some enjoyment in their day on the beach.

It was finally warm enough to risk a dip in the sea and little children hopped over gentle waves with shrieks of delight.

Dads had taken over sandcastle-building and kite-flying duties, seemingly reluctant to let their offspring take a turn, while Mums were setting out the picnics and were on standby to dry shivering children emerging from the waves, swamping them with enormous beach towels. Even in these days of equal opportunity, it seemed that that gender roles were still traditionally defined at the seaside.

Naturally, the great British windbreak was standing proud up and down the beach in significant number. Maria fondly remembered her own father from long-ago seaside holidays in his daily quest for a large stone to hammer in the windbreak poles. Frustratingly, on sandy Dorset beaches they were in short supply.

Maria went downstairs, slipped on her shoes and stepped straight out onto the shingle from her private path. Walking down to the grey shape, she was surprised that it was a small porpoise; such a rare sight on the south coast. About a metre long, its lower jaw was torn and bloodied, but otherwise she couldn't see any other injuries. The last, and only, time she had seen a porpoise was many years ago, swimming between the two Brighton piers. Thomas had been distracted from his metal detector – a much longed-for birthday present – and was yelling "Shark! I can see a shark!" up the beach, much to the consternation of all around.

Watching the creature's curving movements over the waves, a small fin cutting the surface, Maria thought it was a small dolphin at first, but the colouring was too dark. It was definitely a porpoise, happily entertaining the watchers on the beach to an acrobatic display and allowing a group of canoeists get quite close before it swam off towards the Palace Pier.

Showtime over, Thomas went back to his metal detecting, finding a necklace and about £3.50 in loose change before the day was out.

As Maria's first day ended, the sun set dramatically in a burst of pinks and mauves over the empty beach. Seagulls were still looping and calling, although their cockle-fest was over until the tide went out again.

A not quite full moon appeared over the sea as night fell and the path of light it cast led a comforting path straight up to the beach house.

Daniel, are you coming back to me?

*

Disappointingly, sunshine had been replaced by dull grey cloud cover next morning. Maria thought that the day would have a more typically English seaside feel about it. Oh well, yesterday's warmth was a bonus.

There was no sign of the little porpoise as she walked along the deserted beach after breakfast. The out-going tide had left behind a delta-like network of rivulets in the sand and some quite substantial natural paddling pools.

Further along the beach she saw a goodly crowd of people standing around the water's edge. Francesca had told her that a world-famous and particularly handsome A-list actor had been filming on this beach the week before, prompting great interest from the local female population. Perhaps he was back for a retake?

Maria stepped up a gear as she hurried along the beach towards the crowd in the hope of getting a photo or autograph – or both. However, as she drew closer, she could see that small children far out-numbered the adults and there was none of the expected paraphernalia that would accompany a Hollywood film crew.

It was a school activity trip to the beach. (Wearing no make-up and with her hair dishevelled by the brisk sea breeze, in retrospect she really wasn't looking her best to meet a film star.)

The children, all sensibly wearing high visibility vests, were engrossed in picking up shells and bits of sea creatures left by the tide. One boy was chasing a group of screaming little girls with a large crab claw.

Smiling to herself, Maria thought that's exactly what

Daniel would have done in a similar situation.

Taking their lead, Maria began to look for shells and anything else of interest as she walked back along the beach. She had always loved beachcombing and rock-pooling when she was young – and not so young. The children often recalled with great hilarity an incident involving their mother and a rock pool whilst on holiday in Lanzarote. In a reversal of parent/child roles, Francesca was sunbathing, reading a book while Maria delved around in deep pools left behind on the rocky shore at low tide. Such was her concentration in the abundant marine life, she didn't see the slippery algae and went base over apex into the water. Thomas and Daniel were quite impressed by the massive bruises that quickly appeared on her hip and arm, showing that it wasn't just her pride that had suffered. At least nothing was broken; air ambulance back to Gatwick wouldn't have been very dignified.

The morning went quickly and soon Maria was having lunch back at the beach house, followed by her now habitual siesta.

When she awoke, a strange intermittent sound could be heard outside. It sounded like a cow lowing mournfully and it took her a while to realise that it was the foghorn. Peering round the drapes, she saw that a dense sea-fret had rolled in, masking everything more than a few metres from the beach house in pale grey mist. She was glad that she'd been able to get her walk and beachcombing done in the morning and was going to be quite happy just to read, listen to music or sit in peaceful contemplation for the rest of the afternoon.

However, once again the capricious nature of the English weather caught her out and by the time she made a cup of tea, the sea-fret was evaporating and the sun was beginning to burn the clouds away. The tide was a long way out and all Maria could see was acres of wet sand. She people-watched as the sun tempted holiday-makers and locals onto the beach.

Late afternoon, and the sea was rushing in again over the vast expanse of flat beach. Many unsuspecting holidaymakers must have been caught out by how rapidly the tide encroached, ending up with soggy picnics, wet clothes and sodden windbreaks to transport home. Their cars must have had a lingering tang of the sea for weeks afterwards.

Dogs seem to have so much fun on the beach, charging up and down to retrieve balls thrown by their owners; dashing in and out of the waves.

Maria saw a little Westie having the time of his life, running round and round, meeting and greeting other canine visitors to the beach and wondered, had they had lived near the coast when their dog was alive, if she too would have enjoyed days on the beach. She felt a bit guilty for never having let her dog splash in the sea or run on wet sand to fetch a ball. However, seeing how hard the owner had to work to coax and cajole this one back on the lead, maybe it was just as well. Their dog, although sweet-natured and affectionate, had had a very stubborn streak and could be quite wilful at times; it wouldn't have been easy to call time on her fun and games on the beach.

*

As she drank her tea on the last morning before leaving the beach house, Maria noticed that around the open fireplace in the living room, previous holiday guests had written their names on pebbles and added them to the small stones which decorated the hearth. What a lovely idea. She stepped down onto the beach and quickly found a large, smooth pebble to do the same, for she knew that she would return to the beach house time and time again – maybe with grandchildren one day. They would have fun looking for granny's pebble in the hearth and would no doubt want to add their own.

Maybe over the years, they would come to the beach house with their children and grandchildren; more pebbles would be added to the family collection.

Generations of pebbles would appear; continuity of self and of those to whom she had been a daughter, a sister, a wife, a mother… a mother with three children.

She had made a difference and there was hope beyond life.

To be continued